The
Kelly Finger-McNeela Story

I Can & I Did!

One woman's courageous pursuit of a
full life despite battling multiple sclerosis!

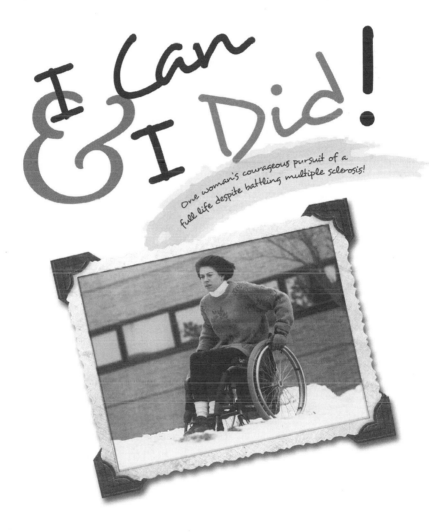

BY DOREEN RICKERT-RADEMACHER

I Can & I Did!
Copyright ©2013 by Doreen Rickert-Rademacher

Doreen Rickert-Rademacher
Email: drademacher@comcast.net
Visit www.icanidid.com for more information and to order a copy of this book.

Special credit and thanks to the Lansing State Journal and photographer Greg DeRuiter for the use of the cover photograph of Kelly in her wheelchair on a snowy sidewalk.

Special thanks to Paws with a Cause for the use of the photo of Kelly with Nori.

Special thanks to Becca Usher for the hours devoted to the photography to make this story come alive. And to Angela Klinske for the tender touch while editing—you made this book so much better!

ISBN: 978-0-9887728-0-9

Printed in the United States of America

Table of Contents:

Dedication:

To my good friend Kelly:
This is your story. Thank you for letting me tell it. Your honesty, candor and brilliant courage enabled me to complete this book and inspired me to make some very big personal changes.

You are so full of life; you virtually sparkle with it and that makes you stand out. Right from the beginning of our friendship, I saw a glimmer of mischief in your eyes and the ghost of a smile on your lips as you prepared to deliver the perfect punch line—always worth waiting for.

The positive impact you've had on my life is immeasurable. Your wit entertains, your perseverance inspires and your determination is formidable.

I'm blessed to know you and I love you like a sister!

Foreword:

O
ne of the first times I met Kelly Finger-McNeela, I saw it... that something special glimmering behind her snapping blue eyes. I readily admit that I was a bit uncomfortable initially, having no experience with disabilities and wheelchairs, not to mention multiple sclerosis. But Kelly has a way of putting people at ease, and I was no exception.

We were enjoying a ladies lunch out, a Tuesday tradition established years ago with good friends who came to be known as the Belmont Moms because that's the town we live in. Outings were orchestrated by Kelly's good friend, Kim Healy. On this particular occasion, I was seated next to Kelly and we had both ordered raspberry lemonade—the house feature at a swanky restaurant on the northeast side of Grand Rapids, Michigan. Uncertainly, I raised her glass and offered her a sip like I had observed others do at previous gatherings. Kelly had lost the use of her arms and hands one year prior. She gave the straw a good slurp but was surprised by the chunks of raspberry that nearly choked her. She coughed and struggled to swallow but as she settled, she grinned at me, adding, "It'd be better with a shot of vodka!"

I knew in that moment that I had met a very special individual. As our friendship grew, I realized that her story needed telling and that it would inspire many others.

Picture this: You wake up one morning, in no rush to get anywhere— there's nothing on your calendar for the day. Then, unexpectedly, your husband comes home; you're still in bed because after all…there was nothing on your calendar. Surprise is mirrored on your face to see him and you feel glad. Then he starts hustling you around to get dressed but won't say why. At that point you hear your parents' voices in your living room. "Hmmm,—that's odd," you think to yourself. Suddenly, you panic, thinking something bad has happened and you immediately worry about your beloved grandmother, who's been ill. Your husband says your grandmother is fine and takes you to the living room. Then he tells you that he can't take care of you anymore and you are going to a nursing home. Today. Of course, you first need to visit a doctor who determines that you have diminished mental capacity (who wouldn't under such tremendous duress), and you find yourself committed to a nursing home, an institution full of the elderly who can no longer care for themselves. There is nearly no one your age, your disease is uncommon and you don't have a friend nearby. Although you are surrounded by other residents (most of them screaming for help, in the clutches of dementia, at all hours of the day and night), you are abandoned, completely unable to help yourself because you're trapped in your own body.

1 From the Start— a Family Legacy

Kelly Marie Finger was born December 13, 1970 at Butterworth Hospital in Grand Rapids, Michigan. Her parents, Linda and Ron, brought her home to an apartment, positioned conveniently above the family business, Fingers Restaurant. Kelly's smile is broad as she describes the family dog, Cocoa, and how he would stand on his hind legs, peering into the basinet from all angles to determine what this new addition was.

Fingers Restaurant was owned by her paternal grand-parents and was a landmark in the greater Grand Rapids area for many years. The restaurant was opened in 1946 in an old farmhouse just off Plainfield Avenue on the city's northeast side; it grew to more than 600 seats and became Kelly's father's family legacy.

Living above the business may sound convenient but Kelly said that it didn't really work out for her parent's marriage. By the time Kelly was two years old, her parents had split up and her mother, Linda, moved with Kelly to Belding, Michigan—Linda's home town, located 20 miles east of Grand Rapids.

"I had left my job in fashion merchandising at Wurzburg's (another landmark business in downtown Grand Rapids) to work in the restaurant after we married in 1968," said Linda. "We lived in an apartment above the restaurant; there was no kitchen, very little privacy and even the washer and dryer were located inside the restaurant. Because it was a family business, Ron was working all the time, it was difficult, and he met someone new. I returned to Belding and while it was a sad time, I did get to keep the rocking chair I had insisted we buy when Kelly was born and that gave me some comfort."

Linda and Kelly moved in with Linda's father, who had recently split from his own wife. A rather unusual family unit, the three of them lived together for five years, and Kelly's grandpa often watched her while Linda worked as a waitress. Linda's sister, Renee, helped out too and often kept Kelly overnight when Linda worked late shifts.

"It was hard, raising Kelly mostly on my own, making ends meet and worrying about things like paying for insurance," said Linda. "In addition to waitressing, I started working at a flower shop down the street, did even more catering and then started working in the school cafeteria—to be involved with Kelly's education."

Eventually, Linda and Kelly moved into an apartment.

"I know it was a good move for my mother. She needed to get us out on our own," Kelly said. "But I had to change schools in the third grade and at the time, I thought it was the end of the world."

As it turned out though, Kelly made some of the best, long-standing friendships of her lifetime thanks to that move.

One of her best friends is Traci Machinchick; the two forged a relationship at the tender age of eight. Tracy would eventually move away—25 miles down the road to Lowell, but that wouldn't stop the friendship and they remained close. Traci attended Kelly when she married and often visits Kelly at her current home—convenient now that Kelly is also in Lowell.

"I was shy and didn't have many friends when Kelly started at my school in third grade," Traci said. "So I went over and offered to play. We had a lot in common, my parents

---

were divorced too, and it was nice going to visit at Kelly's house. She was an only child and things just seemed calmer there. I did a lot of first-time things with Kelly…like eating chicken nuggets and Chinese food. Kelly was the pickiest eater ever! She was always busy, never sat still and we had so much fun. We were pretty much inseparable after that."

Self-described as a quiet, sensitive child, Kelly indicates that she was very much the Tomboy. Her fondest memories of childhood include camping with her dad at Lake Mitchell State Park in Cadillac, Michigan and fishing.

"I remember ice fishing with a tip-up pole and catching a Northern Pike that was over 30 inches long," Kelly said. A satisfied smile lights her face—a visible sense of her victory. Kelly is very skilled at communicating emotion through facial expression. Not by choice but rather by necessity.

"Kelly was always a good fisherman and she liked to go out in the boat," Ron recalls. "She baited her own hook and had lots of patience. I remember picking her up from school early one day and I told the office that she had an appointment...with some Bluegills." Ron took a moment to battle back his emotions—this is clearly a poignant memory for him.

"Back then, I used to make fishing poles," he added. "I still have three or four poles in the shed with her name on them."

Although Kelly lived with her mother, she spent at least two days a week with her dad.

"We had a kind of tradition," Ron said. "When I'd pick her up, we'd always stop at Harold's Drive-In in Belding, and we'd get ice cream cones. Kelly liked chocolate and Kelly's dog, Cocoa, always enjoyed getting a cone too."

Kelly had plenty of other interests and music was one of them. When she was in fifth grade, she joined the band. Her instrument of choice—the French horn.

"I picked it because it wasn't the normal clarinet or trumpet," Kelly said. "I wanted to sort of stand out from the crowd. Dumb, I guess."

On the contrary, there is nothing dumb about Kelly or anything she does. Facing a challenge head-on is typical of her "just do it" attitude.

Ultimately, her Tomboy nature took her onto the basketball court and she was reportedly pretty good at it. Her grin is a bit impish and full of confidence as she speaks of it. Ironically though, it was while playing basketball that Kelly first noticed there was something physically wrong.

"I would run down the court and then couldn't seem to stop or turn," she said. "I also had a foot drop that I couldn't control."

"Kelly was really good at basketball; she earned awards like 'Best Player' and other titles during her middle school years," Linda said. "But in eighth grade, she began having some trouble on the court and I just knew something was wrong. Even coming down the steps into our apartment, I recall reminding Kelly to pick her feet up; I could hear one of her feet sort of slapping down as she descended."

"The signs were all there, she stumbled on the court and there were other things too," Ron added. "I knew something was wrong—but I didn't *want* to know it."

The basketball coach's father was the local doctor, so Linda asked the coach to invite him to come to games to watch Kelly and give Linda his opinion. He agreed that there was definitely a problem and sent them to a special doctor.

"I remember that appointment," Linda said. "I could hear the two doctors talking (behind) the door, saying it was probably MS (multiple sclerosis). I remember feeling a terrible, cold tension overtake me at that moment... just thinking of it now—I feel it all over again."

Shortly after, Kelly saw a pediatrician / neurologist. He ordered several tests, including an MRI and then a spinal tap which solidified the MS diagnosis.

"Do you remember the day the space shuttle Challenger blew up?" Kelly asked. "That was the day—January 28, 1986—that I learned I had MS."

Kelly was just 15 years old.

2 What *is* Multiple Sclerosis?

"It was really dumb, but at first, I remember wishing that I would have the worst type of MS," Kelly said. "That way people would notice me."

Be careful what you wish for.

Multiple sclerosis is a progressive disease with no cure. It impacts the central nervous system: the brain, the spinal column and optic nerves. Damage caused by MS leaves scars or lesions along these nerve paths; the process of developing these scars is known as sclerosis, so multiple sclerosis translated means "many scars." Such scarring interrupts the body's ability to send signals along the central nervous system and the result can be permanent nerve damage and disability.

An estimated 2.5 million people worldwide are thought to have some sort of MS, according to the National MS Society. More than 400,000 of those people are in the United States and it hits twice as many women as men. Most are diagnosed between the ages of 15 and 60 years of age. Kelly was on the youngest end of that range.

The National MS Society website explains the four distinct courses that MS follows:

1. **Relapsing-Remitting** (85% of diagnosed people start with this type)—characterized with relapses (attacks of worsening neurologic function) followed by periods of remission in which partial or complete recovery occurs

2. **Primary-Progressive** (Kelly and just 10% of people stricken with MS fall into this category)—characterized by steadily worsening symptoms that occur over time with no break or relapse period

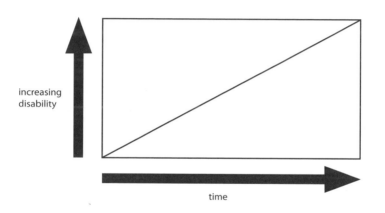

increasing disability

time

3. **Secondary-Progressive**—begins with initial relapsing-remitting followed by progression of disability

4. **Progressive-Relapsing**—the least common and shows progression to disability from the onset followed by acute relapses with or without full recovery.

Although there are treatments to manage the disease course, they are only partially effective, which means that some people's MS will worsen in spite of everything they and their doctors do to try and prevent it. Kelly has experienced this.

At the young age of 15, Kelly was handed a diagnosis that would have emotionally crippled most people. Not Kelly. Although she sought medical advice and pursued treatment, she didn't let the diagnosis stop her from "just being normal."

Two days after having her spinal tap and getting the gloomy diagnosis, Kelly's friend was having a birthday party, and Kelly wasn't about to miss it despite the warnings of the repercussions of a spinal tap.

"I just wanted to be a normal teenager. I didn't think about what was or would be," said Kelly.

She did go to the birthday party and felt fine. However, she encountered one of those side effects the next day.

"The day after the birthday party there was a wrestling match at the high school. My mom was working in the concession area when I got a terrible headache; there were lots of people around to see that," Kelly grimaces as she describes that day.

What Kelly deemed a headache can only truly be appreciated by those that have suffered through a spinal tap—experienced adults report that this sort of headache (also known as post-lumbar puncture headaches) can be completely debilitating.

But, true to her quote, Kelly was committed to being normal and just like any other normal teenage girl, Kelly set out to enjoy the high school experience.

"Well, there were a few boyfriends but two come to my mind—Daniel, the 'Good Guy' and Chris, the 'Bad Boy,'" Linda recollects with the sort of grin a mother can only express in retrospect. "She was with Daniel a lot and I remember when Kelly first told me that he had kissed her...I was driving at the time and nearly jerked the car to a halt! I knew she was growing up, a teenager and all of that, but you're never truly prepared, I guess."

One memorable night gave Linda fits.

"One guy took Kelly out to a party in the boondocks (country slang for somebody's back 40 acres or woods); the cops came and everybody started running," Linda explained. "Well, Kelly couldn't run, so there was that guy trying to help Kelly get away. I was so angry that he would put her in that position!"

Then there was the senior year spring break trip to Florida.

"Once Kelly was diagnosed with MS, I tried to support whatever she wanted to do; I didn't want to stand in her way," Linda said. "I often had to bury my maternal fears—especially hard to do when she and three girlfriends announced they wanted to go to Daytona Beach for Spring Break in Kelly's car. We didn't have cell phones back then; I couldn't possibly keep track of them. I heard stories later of how they ended up in a cornfield somewhere…I still shudder to think of it."

"We were trying to do a U-ie," Kelly said. "We pulled into a cornfield to turn around and got stuck. We had to find somebody to come and tow us out."

Kelly proudly displays the commemorative quilt her mother made from the T-shirts she collected during that trip on her small bed and cherishes the memories of independence. With a grin, she recalls thinking that she knew she had a lot of living to do in what might be a short amount of time. She was anxious to get started and was drawn to what she called the fun, mischievous, "bad stuff."

And she is completely humble as she says, "Well, I was tall and thin with long dark hair so I guess I was OK to look at."

That's an understatement. Kelly was voted homecoming queen of her senior class. Riding onto the football field in a flashy convertible wearing her Grandma Finger's white fur, she literally sparkled!

Kelly smiles and mentions that she was assured that it wasn't a sympathy vote; however, having MS made the evening a bit more interesting.

"I almost fell as I stood up when they announced my name but the homecoming king caught me by the elbows," Kelly said.

She excelled and indeed, stood out, in High School. Voted a Leader and Most Popular in her class, Kelly also performed a part in a skit for the Band Follies with friends and served as secretary and treasurer of the Student Council.

"When it came to activities and events, I had plenty of ideas and *just made it happen*," she said.

Kelly just described her personal mantra.

"I've often thought that Kelly's high school class was special…they had Kelly and another boy, Eddie, who had cancer," Linda explained. "I think the whole class developed a special ability to care. When Kelly graduated and actually walked across the stage, the entire auditorium gave her a standing ovation—Eddie got one too. Several of the kids in that class went on to pursue careers in medicine, nursing, even social work."

It appears that from a very early age, Kelly inspired people around her. And rushing to experience life in a compressed, if unknown, timeframe seemed to drive Kelly unerringly and constantly forward.

3 Heading Out Into the World

E ven before she graduated high school, Kelly decided she wanted to go to college. She applied to Central Michigan University and was accepted soon after. She had also applied to Michigan State University, but that process took longer. She found out she was accepted on Christmas Eve Day.

"I liked CMU but chose MSU because my dad went there and was such a big Spartan fan," Kelly looked off into the distance as she recollected this. "I thought it would make him so proud and happy that I was going to State, like he did. But I'll never forget what his reaction was."

Kelly says that her dad was a bit alarmed by her news and blurted, "How in the hell are you going to get around down there?"

His comment was like a splash of cold water in the face.

"Well, it was definitely a proud moment," Ron said. "But it was scary too. I remember being concerned about how she'd get along because she was already beginning to struggle to walk. When I went to MSU, I sometimes biked 30 minutes to class—how was Kelly going to manage that?"

Undaunted, Kelly applied to James Madison, a residential college at MSU. She moved there in 1989.

"I felt scared, challenged and rebellious," Kelly said. "Every kid going to college is scared. Being on my own was frightening; I was kind of shy and didn't talk a lot. I didn't want to be dependent on my parents but I also remember secretly asking myself, *What the hell was I thinking? Why did I do this?* But I like to be challenged."

The first couple of months were scary for Kelly but after that, she said things were better.

"I think my family would've been happier if I'd stayed home. But after I left, proved to them that I could do it, they were happy. To this day, I'm glad I did it... glad I didn't wuss out and stay home," she explained. "I didn't really consider myself different, I just had unique obstacles."

Kelly wavers and weeps a bit as she drifts from the past to the present. We are talking within the confines of the cur-tained—off room she shares with a dementia patient in a nursing home. It isn't Kelly's choice to be in this place and it's all shockingly new.

"That's probably what makes it so hard to be in here," she sniffed. "I feel that I've just got unique obstacles but it feels like everyone sort of gave up on me."

We take a break while Kelly collects her thoughts and reels in her emotions. Yet another battle she faces - and wins. Later, she tells me that during her time at MSU, Kelly chose to major in Parks and Recreation with an emphasis on Therapeutic Recreation.

"I wanted the major with the longest name," she joked. "I heard about it from a group of people I was playing wheel-chair tennis with in Lansing and I picked it from the list of majors offered at MSU."

"I remember when Kelly first found that group of peo-ple playing wheelchair tennis," Linda said. "They convinced her to try it and that's when her eyes were open to the fact that she could do things, go places. She got this sports wheel-chair...with some financial help from the Belding Rotary and Lions Club; it had a sling for her butt and a strap across the back. She hauled ass all over the place in that thing!"

That's not all Kelly picked up while competing nation-ally with the Greater Lansing Wheelchair Tennis Foundation. Linda said she also got a heart-shaped, floral tattoo during a trip to California with some of the friends she made on the team! Souvenir or rebellion?

When asked about this tattoo—Kelly smiled broadly and offered to show it off.

"I was very proud of that tattoo," she said. "I was glad I got it when I went someplace—as a memory."

"Did I tell you about that trip? It was the time I competed in the U.S Wheelchair Tennis Open in California?" Kelly asked with a snicker. "I got second place in the Women's C Division…there were only two of us competing in it."

"While Kelly was at MSU, she was featured in the college newspaper several times for tennis but also for her independent attitude. I think she met three of the university presidents during her time there," Ron said. "I practically bleed MSU green but I never met any of them!"

After her first year at MSU, Kelly came home for the summer. She had long hair at the time but was due to go visit the Cleveland Clinic for a special Chemo-like treatment in hopes of stalling the progression of her MS symptoms. She and her mother were planning to stay at the Ronald McDonald house in that area.

"Having a place to stay while we were at the Cleveland Clinic was a blessing," Linda said. "The Ronald McDonald House was wonderful; it was very comfortable and was staffed by people that were so helpful and welcoming. They had a sort of chapel area too and boy, did I need that!"

The treatment was grueling and while Kelly couldn't say for sure whether that treatment helped, she did recall heading back to MSU that fall with no hair—partly due to the treatment but mainly because she elected to cut it off.

"They warned me I'd likely lose my hair after the treatment," Kelly said. "I had worn my hair long for several years but it was my decision to cut it off—before it fell out. You've got to do what you can to get by, and make the best of a bad situation."

Our interview is interrupted by a nurse, Beth, who checks on Kelly and it's clear that there is a budding friendship between them.

"Some people who work here don't think I deserve extra time or any more assistance than any other patient," Kelly said. "They don't seem to want to spend time with me. Beth's different—she likes me."

At the heart of the human condition is the need to be liked, cared about and loved. It's often difficult to find when left to depend on employees at a nursing home.

Later, Beth walked me to the restroom (it's a restricted area and she needed to let me into the facility with her key). I commented on how much I appreciate her attention to Kelly and what Kelly has told me. Beth responded:

"I have been with Kelly all along; I was here when her husband brought her here. One day, I saw Kelly in her wheel chair, facing the glass doors. She was just staring out into the courtyard with big tears rolling down her face. I went over to her and said that I didn't know what was happening in her marriage or what had transpired before she came here but that I could see on Brian's face how much he cares and that he is in pain too."

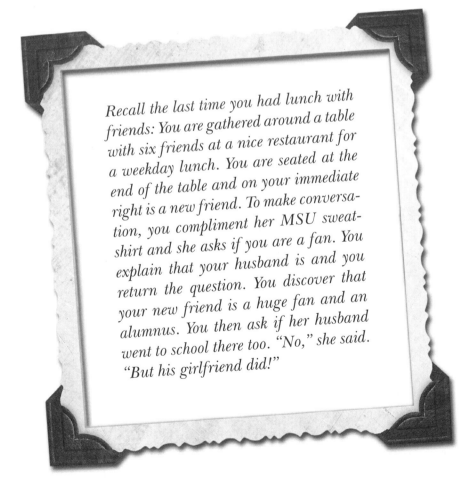

Recall the last time you had lunch with friends: You are gathered around a table with six friends at a nice restaurant for a weekday lunch. You are seated at the end of the table and on your immediate right is a new friend. To make conversation, you compliment her MSU sweatshirt and she asks if you are a fan. You explain that your husband is and you return the question. You discover that your new friend is a huge fan and an alumnus. You then ask if her husband went to school there too. "No," she said. "But his girlfriend did!"

4 Finding Love

B ack at MSU for her sophomore year, Kelly had a new roommate named Heather, from Chicago.

"Heather was a good roommate although she cried a lot," Kelly explained. "I met her boyfriend, Brian McNeela, that year when he came to visit her."

Brian was born on the south side of Chicago on March 30, 1972. He was the youngest of four children born into what he describes as a close-knit, Irish Catholic family.

"My parents emigrated here from Ireland, individually. They met and married here and raised us to work hard, play hard and keep things close to the vest," Brian said. "My mom died when I was seven years old. My brother was nine, my sisters were 11 and 14 and we all worked together to make it. I attended Catholic school and was in the eighth grade when my father remarried. It was... challenging...I moved out immediately after graduation, lived first with my siblings then enrolled at Illinois State University. I lived in my uncle's three-flat basement office. It was basically an 8' x 10' room, very cramped, but I made it there for a year," he added, smiling ruefully. Brian would attend four different community colleges, pursuing engineering and computer science but money was an issue so he opted to go to work at Arthur Andersen, one of the country's Big Five accounting firms at the time. He started in the mail room and eventually advanced to the training department.

"Back in high school, I dated a girl named Heather who eventually went on to MSU and became Kelly's roommate," Brian explained. Grinning, he added, "Heather was a prude; Kelly was always more fun… she drove, drank, smoked—not cigarettes, she was gutsy and cute, a good package."

Kelly recalled one visit, when Brian had his older brother's ID and bought blackberry brandy and cherry Coke.

"We got drunk and Brian decided to push me in my wheelchair down the dorm hallway yelling and knocking on every door," she laughed.

The following spring, Heather dropped out of MSU, went home and eventually broke up with Brian.

That summer, Kelly saw a very special greeting card and sent it to Brian.

"Brian used to tease me about my last name, which was Finger," Kelly said. "So I sent him a birthday card that had a woman on the front with her middle finger up, under the caption 'You're number 1!' He got it and called me…it was November and I told him I had just voted for Ross Perot. He gagged."

Kelly was in the middle of her junior year at MSU and, in a typical rite of passage, had moved off campus. She made a new friend, Amy, and the two of them decided to make a road trip to Chicago for a wheelchair basketball event at the University of Illinois. Coincidentally, Brian's brother attended that college so they all met up.

"We went out to a bar and I was under the impression that Brian liked Amy, so when she asked me, I told her that I didn't like him," Kelly said. "I was protecting myself in case he did like her. But nothing happened between them and a month later, he came to visit me at MSU. We went to the

Peanut Barrel (bar), came back home and talked a lot. You know how sometimes you might compare the size of your hands with someone else's—by pressing palms together? Well, Brian and I did that and I felt that we were getting closer, that he might even kiss me. But that didn't happen, and the next day I took him to the train station."

Before getting on the train, Brian playfully ran across the train tracks—which prompted Kelly to yell at him out of concern. Then he asked her if, on his next visit, they could go out. She said yes. Then he kissed her on the cheek and left.

"Oh, she yelled at me for that too," Brian reported with a wide smile. "She was telling me that I should have kissed her earlier."

"I was still uncertain of the situation," Kelly said. "Was he talking about an actual date or what? I remember wondering why he would like me."

The next time Kelly saw Brian was when she and a friend travelled to Chicago for another wheelchair basketball game.

"I told Kelly that I'd come down to the game to see her," Brian added. "It was a two-hour train ride for me and I sold my junk car for the money to go. After the game, Kelly and her friend gave me a ride back home and they stayed with me that night. It was interesting because there were three steps going down into my apartment. Kelly insisted on walking down them and at one point, I had to help her move one of her legs. I didn't mind. I had been a camp counselor in the past, working with special education kids so it wasn't new to me—working around disabilities I mean."

"Brian cooked us chicken legs and fries in his apartment; then we went out to a bar called the Library. We came back to Brian's place and my friend slept in another room while Brian and I were on the couch. I lounged back against his chest while we were watching 'The Jungle Book,' of all things, and I just chatted away until I realized he had fallen asleep," Kelly said, rolling her eyes.

Kelly found herself travelling to Chicago again soon after that for a Disabled Sports and Recreation conference. That's the line of work Kelly had chosen to pursue, and she stayed with Brian the first night she was in town.

"Brian was in the process of moving but that didn't matter, he invited me to stay and I was anxious to spend time with him, so I did," Kelly said.

After the conference, Kelly drove herself home, in a car she operated with hand controls. Kelly would later go to work for the organization that sponsored the conference, but first she accepted an internship with the Atlanta Paralympic Organizing Committee in 1993.

"I had to move to Atlanta that August. My mom took me but had a hard time leaving me," Kelly said. "I found it extremely exciting and I lived alone for the first time, ever!"

"Well, once Kelly had made up her mind to go to Atlanta, there was no turning back," said Linda. "You just couldn't tell her she couldn't or shouldn't do something—it just didn't fly with her. She'd find a way. The rest of the family was mad as hell and worried because when we set out in a van with a U-Haul trailer bound for Atlanta, we had no idea where Kelly was even going to live. We had to get there first and that proved to be difficult enough—I had trouble navigating the vehicles because I had never towed anything before and we got stuck in a hotel parking area. I couldn't back the thing out! We had to stay overnight and ask for help the next morning!"

Looking back on that trip, Linda chuckled and can now find some humor in it, but she also described a particularly horrific moment.

"Once we found Kelly a safe place to live, we settled her in. It turned out that she was close to accessible public transit and could get around the city alright but life in a wheelchair is daunting," Linda explained. "The elevator she had to use to get on the train took her down into a dark, dank sort of area that made me cringe and even finding a bathroom when you need one is awful."

Linda described a simple shopping trip to buy some essentials for Kelly's apartment. The two women were in a major department store, thinking they'd be able to find Kelly a restroom to use. However, it was located on the third floor and even getting to the elevator was tough—the racks of merchandise were so tightly packed together that maneuvering around them was practically impossible. Then, once they saw the women's restroom, they realized it didn't contain a handicapped accessible stall. The only one was located in the men's room which Linda described as deplorably dirty. Plus, the handicapped stall wasn't big enough.

"It was impossible for her chair to fit in that stall so believe it or not, Kelly actually had to get down on that filthy floor, crawl to the toilet and then pull herself up onto it just so she could go to the bathroom! The challenges were monumental," Linda said, shaking her head. "And when I think back to it, realizing how important it was for her to get out on her own, I'm amazed at the guts it took for her to do it."

"When I heard Kelly planned to move down to Atlanta, I was scared to death—again," Ron said. "I didn't know how she would manage to get around a strange city all alone but you know what? She found a way. She has that 'don't give up' attitude and it's absolutely amazing to me, the things she has accomplished."

Kelly was thrilled and excited to be in Atlanta and truly on her own, but mostly, she was anxious to see Brian again, so she bought him a ticket to Atlanta for Labor Day weekend.

"I wanted to tour Atlanta and thought it would be fun if Brian could see it with me," Kelly said with a telling grin. "We went to Little Five Points which is a hippie place. It was very interesting—there was lots of tie dye!"

Brian came prepared for a special visit, bringing candles and homemade spaghetti sauce to cook dinner with.

"I absolutely loved it," Kelly said. "I was really starting to feel less insecure about our relationship status."

A short few weeks later, Brian flew Kelly back to Chicago to attend a family wedding. He then travelled to Michigan to see Kelly while she was home for Thanksgiving. At Christmas, Kelly was home again so Brian made a return visit. It was also the month Kelly graduated from MSU—December of 1993.

"The graduation ceremony was held on campus, at the Breslin Center. I had a green cap and gown and while it was exciting, I didn't consider it to be that big of a deal—I never doubted that I'd finish what I had started," Kelly explained.

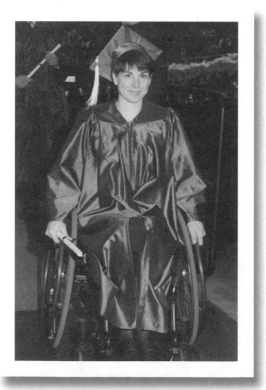

With graduation and her initial internship behind her, Kelly started planning her next step. The degree she had earned required certification involving direct work with people. The Paralympic internship was more of an administrative job so she needed to pursue another. Kelly found such a position at the Rehabilitation Institute of Chicago (RIC) in the spring of 1994.

At RIC, Kelly helped people with strength training and conditioning utilizing the equipment on the physical therapy floor. That summer, one of the part-time employees broke his leg so Kelly was asked to stay on and take over the job. "Once I started working there, things just kind of fell into place," Kelly said slyly. "I was in Chicago and just couldn't wait for Brian so we decided to live in sin."

Brian describes a series of apartments, eventually landing in a place with a fenced-in back yard where the couple could get a dog—they welcomed a golden retriever named Bailey into the relationship.

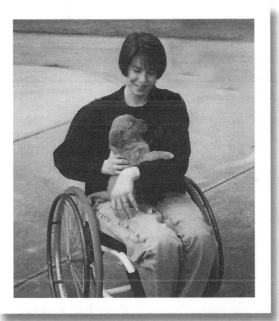

"I always think people should start out with a dog," Kelly said. "It's a little responsibility, but not too much…sort of like practice for having kids."

"Kelly loved that dog and vice versa," Brian reminisced. "Bailey really loved to be under Kelly's chair. Each day, Kelly would roll her chair up against the couch and then get down on the floor of the apartment to stretch. But one day, the chair rolled away into the kitchen, 'damn it' Kelly must have said. Because she would then have to drag herself along the floor over to the chair, push it back to the couch and then climb in. Bailey probably watched her the whole time with what must have been an expression of, 'well, what do you want me to do about it?'".

Unique obstacles?

"There were lots of things like that," Brian explained. "Try waiting 30 minutes for snow to melt off your windshield because you couldn't reach to brush it off from your wheelchair."

Undaunted, Kelly travelled along her career path, determined to be "normal." As far as her relationship with Brian, she didn't think about the future.

"I tried not to think about it," she said. "Because I remember when we were first living together, I dreamily mentioned something to my Grandma Ruth about Brian and I getting married someday and she responded vehemently with an, 'oh, you can't do that to him.' I felt stunned for a moment; that comment made me think that I wasn't worth anything," Kelly frowned as she continued. "I second-guessed myself, thinking, 'what am I doing, I'm just wasting his time.'"

Overcoming doubts expressed by others is something Kelly has continually done and she succeeds by framing her own perspective—she's simply got some unique obstacles, and none of them are big enough to stop her from moving ahead in life and love.

Most couples will have spats from time to time and Kelly described one key situation with her trademark humor.

"The winter I moved in, Brian almost broke up with me," she said. "He wanted to go out with one of his friends (an old girlfriend) but I didn't want to go. He went anyway and came home quite late—after I was already in bed. In a huff the next morning, I packed my stuff to go home for the weekend. In route, my car went off the road. I called my mom and dad - who then called Brian. I hadn't called Brian myself because I wanted him to feel bad." Kelly snickered as she reminisced—just like any other woman scorned. "I had gone off the road and completely through the median," Kelly described. "I did eventually get myself out though– with the help of a big green snow plow truck."

"Brian and I eventually worked things out," Kelly said. "I think he realized that he didn't want to be without me."

The next spat confirmed her feelings.

"It was December and Brian went out with some friends but told me he'd be home early. It was after 2 a.m. and I was pissed," Kelly said. "When he came to the bedroom, he found that I'd tossed his comforter and pillow on the floor so he decided to go sleep on the futon in the front room. The next morning, he crawled into bed and said 'you know I love you, don't you? So will you marry me?' and he showed me a ring. I recognized it immediately—it was my Grandma Finger's wedding ring."

Unbeknownst to Kelly, three months earlier, Brian had made a special trip to see Kelly's Grandma Finger, explaining that he wanted to ask Kelly to marry him. He knew that Grandma Finger had intended for Kelly to someday have her diamond. Grandma Finger immediately removed her own wedding set from her hand and gave it to Brian—happily.

"Well, she did hand it to me right on the spot but I told her to be sure she cleared that with her husband first," Brian smiled. "She actually gave it to me a few weeks later."

Kelly took a long time to answer Brian's proposal of marriage. That old nagging doubt was in the back of her mind; she needed time to think and she phoned a cousin to get another opinion.

"My cousin assured me that Brian must have thought it over and wouldn't have proposed if he didn't want to get married," Kelly said.

"Kelly did take forever to decide," Brian recalled. "Flash forward 15 years to where we are today - what we're facing; that's why. But love is blind."

Eventually, Kelly weighed her own feelings, accepted Brian's proposal and immediately began wearing the ring.

The next weekend, excited to share the happy news, Kelly and Brian celebrated Christmas with her Grandma Ruth's family. Kelly said the prayer over the meal.

"Thank you for our blessings and for everyone coming here today. And I hope you can all make it back to Grand Rapids in the spring, when we're going to get married!"

It's Christmas, the saddest time of the year at a nursing home. Considering the female to male ratio is likely 10—1, you know that most of the residents were wives and mothers themselves and likely played lead roles in making family holiday celebrations special for others. Now, holiday cheer is limited to a few dismal door hangers and shoddy light displays. It's such a sad place. Kelly's spirits are at an all-time low. She is seeing a counselor weekly, she cries often, and is taking an increased dose of anti-depressants. She doesn't even want to get out of her bed for today's interview. Who could blame her? Hoping to find a happy memory to dwell on, I ask her to tell me about her most memorable Christmas.

"When Brian and I were first together, I had a hand mirror. It was old, the handle was broken and sort of sharp," Kelly said, her eyes welled with tears. "Brian noticed that, which touched me so deeply, and he got me a new one for Christmas. It was a simple gift but very meaningful and sweet to me."

5 White Lace, Sequins and Promises

Undeterred by the opinion of others, Kelly and Brian began making their wedding plans shortly after the holiday season of 1995.

"During all of Kelly's challenges with MS, I have only ever seen her crack / breakdown twice," said Linda. "She is incredibly strong and has been through so much - hospitals, needles and painful treatments; she's faced dooming predictions about life with this disease including the news that it wouldn't be a good idea to bear children. She took it all in, stoically. But just a few weeks before the wedding, she fell apart. I found her sobbing in the bathroom, wondering if she was doing the right thing by bringing Brian into all the things she'd have to face."

Kelly got past the doubts and she and Brian did move forward with what Linda describes as a "we'll deal with it when we face it" sort of attitude.

The actual wedding date was set for May 11, 1996, primarily based on the availability of reception space at the Hilton Spinnaker on 28th Street in Grand Rapids. What bride hasn't faced the dilemma of finding a church and a reception hall available on the same date?

"I just got out the yellow pages and started dialing," Kelly smiled and said. "That's how I got my photographer too and then I started looking for a dress."

Kelly knew exactly the style of dress she wanted, of course!

"I was always sort of thin so I wanted a straight dress that was off the shoulders and had fitted arms. Plus, I wanted a little flash," she said, adding that her dress did have beading and some sequins but she absolutely couldn't see herself wearing a bustle. She concluded that statement by sticking out her tongue for emphasis.

"I found my perfect dress," Kelly explained. "It was expensive and originally priced at $1,500 but I got it for $300 because the zipper had to be fixed." Getting a good deal always puts a special twinkle in Kelly's eye!

"To stay on budget, Brian and I tried to do most of the work for the wedding ourselves," she said. "We did have lots of help, even though we didn't ask for it, and that made it even more special."

While most brides might choose a church for the beauty of its stained glass or based on a family tradition, Kelly picked Aldersgate Methodist Church in northeast Grand Rapids for one very unique reason—it had no stairs.

"I could still stand up—with some help, but for the most part I was using a rigid-framed wheelchair by that time so steps were out of the question," Kelly said.

Brian and Kelly had two officiates perform the wedding conjunctly. Brian is Catholic so there was a priest, and Kelly's mom was close friends with a female minister.

"It went well," Kelly explained. "We had about 225 guests and a large wedding party full of siblings and life-long friends."

Kelly had chosen light pink for her five bridesmaids and had a harpist play during the ceremony. Fortunately, another close friend of her mother had the talent to play beautifully, making the event unique.

"Yeah, then after the ceremony, the whole wedding party got onto a big old purple bus to head over to the reception," Kelly giggled and added that during the evening, to get the bride and groom to kiss, the guests had to sing a song with "love" in the title.

"We heard everything from Barney to Jesus Loves You. It was cute and fun," she said.

Music always plays a memorable part of weddings and Brian and Kelly chose their special music carefully.

"Our first dance, complete with me in a wheelchair, was to 'Love' by Nat King Cole," Kelly said. "Our attendants joined us for the Randy Travis ballad, 'Forever and Ever, Amen' and I had my daddy-daughter dance to 'The Way You Look Tonight' originally by Frank Sinatra".

The couple stayed right at the hotel for their wedding night which Kelly described as great but laughed as she described how funny her bottom looked after taking off her dress.

"I had all these popcorn-y shaped indentations on my butt from sitting on my beaded dress; not all that sexy, I guess," she added with a shrug.

Then it was off to the perfect honeymoon destination... Disney World.

"We chose Disney because I knew I could get around easily, it's definitely wheelchair accessible," Kelly said. "Plus, Brian has a goofy, sort of Mickey Mouse personality so I thought it'd be fun."

Mickey Mouse?

"Well, yeah, he's outgoing, silly and talks a lot. He doesn't take things too seriously and is the life of the party," Kelly explained. "I was definitely star-struck, in love and felt very confident with him."

Imagine this: You are a hard-working husband, building a career, maintaining a home, loving your wife and raising a daughter along with numerous pets. Professionally, it's a dog-eat-dog world; you often work long hours and have to travel on occasion. It is getting harder and harder to function because you haven't had a full night's sleep in more than five years. Coming home should be a respite from the workday but for you, it simply means resuming your second job…caring for your wife because she is incapacitated by her MS. You know she can't help it—that she would give almost anything to be independent again—but it's gotten to the point that she can't be left alone during the day. She can't bathe or feed herself, and although she hates relying on others, you must attend to even the most basic of her needs.

6 On Our Way

B ack in Chicago, the newlyweds settled into married
life. But another Paralympic opportunity was knocking
on Kelly's door and she didn't hesitate to take it. This
time around, Kelly had a chance to actually participate in the
Paralympics as the Team Manager for the sitting volleyball
team. She had no worries about where to live this time—she
bunked with the athletes in the Olympic Village—an experience very few people ever get to have!

"It's like the Olympics for people with disabilities," Kelly
explained. "For example, the players on the sitting volleyball
team needed to have one cheek on the floor when contacting
the ball! The Olympic village was very hilly and spread out.
It was an exciting venue and a neat opportunity."

Linda recalled attending opening ceremonies in the
Olympic Stadium, saying "Brian and I went to Atlanta to see
the ceremony and saw Kelly come out along with the athletes
and parade around the circle. Mohamed Ali participated and
it was unbelievable...I was so incredibly proud of her."

Kelly found it hard to be away from Brian; however, and she was ready to head home to Chicago after the games closed. A few months later, Kelly and Brian began discussing a move home—to Michigan.

"One night, we were just coming home and heard a scream; Brian saw a kid running by with a gun and we later learned of a murder in our neighborhood," Kelly said with a distasteful look on her face. "Moving back to Michigan had been in the back of our minds. At that time, I was still self-sufficient and didn't need help from anyone but there were pros and cons to staying in Chicago. That shooting made the cons outweigh the pros."

"Yeah, there were gang bangers—this was Chicago after all," Brian elaborated. "But it was more about Kelly's health; I knew she was getting worse so I asked her about moving back to Michigan. We packed it up and moved home with nothing but $1,000 and the dog."

Neither had employment at the point of moving but they found a warm welcome and moved in with Kelly's dad for a while.

"We ate like kings," Brian laughed, referencing the family restaurant background of course!

Kelly described that time as making a huge leap of faith.

It paid off though and Brian shortly found work at White & White Pharmacy as a parts guy for wheelchairs.

"I sold some and fixed some," Brian nods. "Then a job opened up at BDO Seidman in the mail room so I started there and worked my way up. Now I'm in the IT department as a business system analyst. I talk to various departments (people) who need website help and act as a liaison to the developers."

Eventually, the short stay with Kelly's dad would end and the couple moved to Kelly's home town—Belding.

"My Grandma Ruth and her husband had renovated a home for us. It was a nice place with laminate and hard surface floors, all on one level and we were there for about six years," Kelly said.

Kelly was successful at finding work too and she joined the staff at the Saint Mary's Living Center located near 4 Mile Road and Alpine Ave. in Grand Rapids. She was the Activity

Director and performed evaluations, managed admissions and planned activities.

She was able to drive herself to work and liked the job. But within a year, MS would begin to affect her optic nerve, causing her eyes to jump and rendering her unable to drive. She and Brian compensated by car pooling and Brian would drop her off and pick her up daily.

Kelly and I concluded our interview to plan our next session—we agreed to discuss how the couple decided to start a family. I asked for permission to record the next session; I suspected Kelly's daughter, Rylee, may want to have that at some point in the future. Kelly agreed and I expressed apprehension at the thought of having to master a recently purchased piece of recording equipment and the accompanying software. Kelly surprised me by impatiently rolling her eyes and telling me to "just do it". There's a lesson for all of us in that simple but very profound statement!

7 Starting a Family

After being married for a couple of years, Kelly began thinking about children.

"My friend was pregnant and had this really big belly," Kelly said. "She shared her experience with me and it was sort of like going through it personally but I felt so sad. Physically, it just wasn't smart for me to attempt a pregnancy. I knew it was the next step—to have a child, and I started thinking about adoption."

The same friend knew a woman who had recently adopted a child from Guatemala. So Kelly turned to the same resource, Adoption Associates, for help in the fall of 1998.

"When Kelly started talking about adoption, she said it was my decision," Brian said. "I was never good at saying 'no' to Kelly so we proceeded with our application. That's a decision I will never regret; Rylee is one of the best things that has ever happened in my life."

In January, the couple made the first of two required trips to Guatemala. They met the infant that would eventually become their daughter. She was three months old at the time and both Brian and Kelly were excited about the prospect of really getting to take her home at some point in the future.

"We picked Guatemala because it seemed like the most westernized city," Brian said. "But it was quite an experience because while they had places like Schlotsky's Deli, we saw kids eating there, dressed in fatigues and carrying M16 rifles."

The adoption process in Guatemala involves two steps so Brian and Kelly had to return to Michigan to await final approval and to prepare.

"We went home, got a bed for her and got the room ready," Kelly beamed. "My mom painted a mural on the nursery wall with fish and coral. It was beautiful. She is a terrific artist (I've always been a 'wannabe') and it meant a lot to me to have her do that."

Over the next few months, Kelly's job was reduced to part time and eventually, expectations were changed to include tasks that Kelly could no longer accomplish. While that left her without work, she was filled with hope and anticipation.

"Within a few days of leaving my job, I got the call from Adoption Associates about our baby," Kelly said. "So I called to ask Brian if the time was right and he said yes!"

On July 4, 2000, the couple travelled back Guatemala. Linda went along to help.

"The very next day, the child's foster mother brought her to us," Kelly recollected. "It was like a dream becoming reality. She had lots of hair and was wearing a red dress over a white shirt and little white thigh-high socks! She was happy at first but then became upset and the only thing that would sooth her was Brian walking her around the hotel room."

The new baby was named Alejandra Maria by her birth mother but Kelly and Brian wanted to give her a name that would represent her new family. They selected Marie for her middle name because that's Kelly's middle name and Linda's too. They chose Rylee for her first name because it's definitely Irish which represents Brian's heritage, but the unique spelling also ties to Kelly's father, Ron Lee Finger.

Linda lights up when asked about bringing Rylee home. "It was pure pleasure for me to go along on the trip to Guatemala and help Kelly and Brian bring her home; such a blessing."

"I did have some doubts," Kelly said. "I felt bad about not giving Brian a child of his own, with his DNA, but he told me that it didn't matter and joked that Rylee was cuter than any offspring he'd produce."

Back in Belding, they made some special accommodations so that Kelly could manage with Rylee. "Brian rigged up a changing table that was sort of low so I could reach from my chair," Kelly said. "I had a lot of help though from my neighbor Marguerite and a friend—Julie. We couldn't have done it without them."

"I've heard it said that it takes a village to raise a child but with MS, it takes an entire city," Brian said.

"Rylee was already nine months old when we came home; she had teeth and was on the verge of crawling," Kelly said. "We were so worried about our dog Bailey and the possibility that Rylee might be allergic but there were no problems. It was so cute to see them together—Rylee called Bailey 'Bo.'"

"By the time she was 3 years old, Rylee had the thickest hair, it was very curly and long—way down to her butt," Brian said. "Kelly wouldn't cut it—she just loved it! She found motherhood to be very fulfilling; it gave her something to strive for, for a long time."

Brian paused for a moment in the interview and seemed to be collecting his thoughts. Then he added "Rylee really likes to watch home videos of that time, but I have to leave the room; I can't watch, it reminds me of what Kelly was— fun and independent. It's just too painful to remember."

8 A Very Special House

The time came to leave Belding when Rylee was three. Brian and Kelly considered different communities, eventually selecting Belmont and a property deal that included the building site and a contracted builder.

"I always felt that I wanted to live beyond Belding," Kelly said. "I knew we'd fit in better nearer the faster pace of Grand Rapids; I've always had big ambition and wanted to experience as much of life as I could."

That ambition and energy turned out to be fortuitous as they broke ground for their new home. This was no cookie-cutter floor plan- it was a unique project, including complete access for Kelly's wheelchair and amenities to make daily living much easier. The entrance was graded for direct access— no stairs allowed, and there was a ramp built into the garage. They installed a 4" raised tub and toilet from the get-go and had to order extra heavy-duty lumber to build an elevator in the center of the house. This was a first for their builder.

Kelly took special pride in decorating the home in eye-pleasing warm neutrals accented with plenty of MSU green.

Rylee got to choose her own bedroom colors too. This was a happy time for the McNeela family.

There was also another addition to the family—a service dog named Nori. A beautiful golden retriever chosen for her loyal and soft temperament, Kelly was grateful to get her.

"When Brain told me that he had applied for a service dog with a Michigan-based organization known as Paws for a Cause, I thought I'd never need one," Kelly said. "But, two years later, when my name came up, I was ready. I know it made Brian feel more comfortable leaving me alone too. Nori kept me independent and mobile longer, plus I'd take her for walks and care for her—it gave me purpose, it got me out there more and it gave me a sense of security—that I wasn't alone."

9 Elementary My Dear—Life's a Party!

At the local elementary school, people simply got used to seeing Kelly and Nori in the hallways, and everyone enjoyed it when Nori came to the classroom. This duo was in the classroom often too because Kelly was committed to being involved in Rylee's education as well as the classroom parties.

Kelly acted as the head room parent during Rylee's fourth grade year. And according to Rylee, she was amazing at it.

"Our fourth grade class always had the best parties," Rylee said. "I knew because I looked into the other classrooms and saw the kids playing the old bingo games and the regular stuff. But my mom came up with neat stuff like attaching a tennis ball to a racquet and competing to see who could bounce it on the racquet the most times—there were always prizes and it was cool."

Kelly must have made the fourth- grade teacher's life much easier by handling the details of the seasonal parties because Kelly still carries a hand-made purple blanket that was given to her by that teacher.

"There's a note sewn onto one of the corners of the blanket," Kelly said, directing me to find it. It reads: Thank you for making our year fun! It is signed: Mrs. Guy's Fourth Grade Class.

There are other remnants from those fourth grade parties still floating around too.

"One of the things my mom did at one party was to divide us into teams—she even had team sweatbands made for us to wear," Rylee said. "Just recently, I saw a classmate wearing one of those sweatbands and we're in the seventh grade now."

Good Friend, Kim Healy, helped out in one of the other fourth grade classrooms and conceded that Kelly indeed has tremendous party planning skills!

"There isn't anything Kelly wouldn't try... she was always thinking of ways for those kids to have a great time and she never ran out of ideas," Kim commented. "During our elementary years, I came to know her as just another mom around school who wanted to connect with other women and to raise good, strong kids."

Whatever the school activity was, Kelly wanted to be there.

"She always wanted to make things better for me...to be sure I was having a good time," Rylee said. "Like the end-of-the-year talent show for example, even if I wasn't in it, she wanted to come."

Adults enjoyed Kelly's party planning creativity too.

"I remember Kelly calling me, asking us if we were available to come over for a party she was planning," said friend, Natalie Kleis. "Then, we got information in the mail about this being a murder/mystery party and we had roles to play in it. We went out and got costumes, I was supposed to come as Dianna Rush, and we acted out this play to figure out who had committed the murder. It was so much fun! I remember thinking that here's this woman, stuck in a wheelchair and you'd think she couldn't do much. But she orchestrated everything and made sure that we all had a good time—impressive!"

Kelly also instigated several block parties in the neighborhood complete with township fire trucks and DJs. But years fly by and MS doesn't relent.

"My mom was always the best block party planner—she usually organized everything," Rylee said. "The township sent fire trucks over here and they'd open the fire hydrants and everything. I really liked having so many people come to that party and being with everyone."

By the time Rylee was in fifth grade, Kelly had lost the use of all limbs and extremities. She began using a catheter, a feeding tube and operated her power wheelchair with an apparatus she could push on with her lower jaw.

"There was a long lapse between visits to the neurologist at this point," Kelly said. "I guess it was due to lack of hope; it seemed like every time I'd go in, they'd say they were sorry but there was nothing they could do for me."

Despite the lack of encouraging news or treatment options, Kelly just refused to look backward or to grieve the functionality she had lost.

"First of all, I tried to stay positive. I never wanted people to say 'oh that poor girl' or any other sort of sympathetic comment," Kelly said. "I didn't spend time worrying about what I'd lost; I always looked forward and had the attitude of dealing with what came next, when it came. Sure, I've wondered what it would be like if I didn't have MS, but you can't do anything about it! So when people ask if I've seen the latest research on this drug or that treatment, I tell them that I choose to spend my energy living."

"I sometimes wonder what it would be like if my mom didn't have this disease—to see her up walking around and making lunches and stuff," Rylee commented. "But ever since I was young, as far back as I can remember, she was in a wheelchair and she lost the use of her arms gradually so that we adjusted, it was normal. If I had known her when she could walk around and everything, I'd probably miss it."

Living with MS must seem strange to a child and comprehending exactly what is happening can be challenging for most adults.

"I found some books on MS in our basement one time," Rylee explained. "There was one about what to do if your parent has MS and it was a bunch of stories told by kids. I remember one boy's story and how he would get angry at people who would stare at his mom and he'd tell them she's just as normal as anyone else. I feel that way too...when people stare, it's just so rude."

Rylee does have some great, if unique, memories from her early years and recalls a story about a time when her mom had to get a new wheelchair—the power, motorized, chair she is in now.

"I'd get in mom's old chair and we'd race down the street to the end of the cul-de-sac," Rylee said. "We had a lot of fun... Mom always made the best of it. She doesn't give up and that's the great thing about her, she's a big participator in everything. And my friends—they love her! I remember when my friend, Bailey, gave me a t-shirt with a phrase on it about curing MS—she had it printed for me! I don't care if it doesn't fit anymore...I'll keep that forever."

Picture yourself as a normal 12-year-old girl, constantly on your cell phone, texting friends and frolicking with your puppy, Daisy. You love music, soccer, snowboarding and your parents. As most girls do, you have had some tense moments with your mom lately...it's just like the mother-daughter angst we've all heard about. She is trying to tell you what to do, like you are still a child and you're trying to prove that you're grown up. You want to do what you want to do, when you want to do it. It's all about independence at this stage. But, there's the little part of you that still craves the childhood comforts...like lying alongside your mom at bedtime, stretched out just to relax and talk about whatever comes up. You really enjoy joking around with her because you have a similar sense of humor and you love to beat her at the memory word games she likes to play.

You have a fondness for telling one story in particular about the time you when you were quite young and you climbed up on your mom's bed right after she had been given some medication and was sort of loopy / silly. You asked her: "What does Goofy say? Nothing... he's a dog!"

How do You Know When it's Time?

10

"**W**hen I met Kelly she was walking. When we married, she was driving. When we adopted Rylee, she was in a wheelchair," Brian outlined succinctly.

He is reserved, even a bit apprehensive to discuss the events that led up to moving Kelly into a nursing home. He asked if I'd throw him under the bus.

Brian mentions the evolving role he has played in Kelly's life. Going from lover/husband to caregiver in as few as five years has undoubtedly left him reeling, but he mentions that it was a gradual shift, always requiring just a little more.

"It probably started with my impatience and Kelly's advancing condition," Brian said. "She was always independent, but her tasks were taking longer and longer so I did more and more."

As an example, Brian mentioned the three or four trips to the bathroom Kelly needed each night. At first, Kelly could still get out of bed- it was a struggle for her but she could do it. It might take Kelly 30 minutes to get to the bathroom and back. Brian stepped in to help because his effort could accomplish the task in five minutes. The downside, of course, was lack of consistent sleep for him over the course of several years.

When Kelly began using a catheter, the nighttime ritual eased somewhat, but Kelly still needed to be turned three or four times each night.

"Kelly can still move her head and during sleep she does that a lot. So the many pillows she uses get knocked askew and they need adjusting, repeatedly."

The gradual increase in Kelly's need for assistance was slow and each modest adjustment simply became the new normal.

"Brian made it seem like it was no big deal, helping me," Kelly said. "So I just learned to think it was OK. I never wanted anyone to have to take care of me."

In a typical day, back in 2006, Brian would get Kelly up at 5:30 am, help her shower, dress her and put her in her chair. He'd get ready for work, get Rylee up and ready for school. Eventually, after much persuasion, Kelly agreed to allow aides to come in to help with the morning routine. Kelly initially resisted that.

"It took a lot of convincing," Brian said. "The things the aides need to do are pretty intimate."

Personal grooming is something many people take for granted. The cutting of finger and toe nails, cleaning of ears and nose, brushing teeth and hair, shaving legs and arm pits are just the basics that Kelly had to rely on Brian for. Not to mention dealing with monthly menstruation, urine bags and bowel movements.

Soon thereafter, Brian sought legal assistance and got a Medicaid Waiver which allowed home health aides to come in 16-32 hours per week. Over the course of a few years, the hours increased to 36 per week. This provided for aides to stay with Kelly through the day and then after school, Brian relied on a plethora of people to help.

Brian simultaneously worked to advance his career.

Increasing responsibility at work included a growing workload which often spilled over into evening hours. But before he could get to that, he saw to dinner, homework and extracurricular activities for Rylee, and he put Kelly to bed around 8 pm each night.

By the summer of 2009, Kelly couldn't be left alone.

"A few times, I'd come home and find that Kelly's head had fallen off to the side of her wheelchair head rest and she'd be stuck hanging off, her neck strained and looking straight up at the ceiling. She had no way of picking up her own head and the dog couldn't help either."

Brian hesitated to leave Rylee alone with Kelly.

"A family member had indignantly mentioned that Rylee could take some time to be with her mother," Brian explained. "But what impact would it have on Rylee if something happened to Kelly while Rylee was in charge? That's no position to put a child in."

That pressure escalated to the point where Brian said his own health was suffering. The proverbial straw that broke the camel's back came in 2010.

"I got sick," Brian stated matter-of-factly. "I had a cough for over six months, it was stress related, and some friends told me to do something about it or they were going to call my brother."

That night, Brian sat down and decided to email his brothers and sisters. They jumped to Brian's aid in a matter of hours—a strong show of support from that close-knit family.

Unbeknownst to Kelly, Brian's family helped him to build a committee of advisors to get him through the tough decision-making he faced. There was much to consider.

"I consulted with a doctor, a counselor, a nurse and even a school psychologist / counselor for Rylee," Brian said. "I had spoken with a lawyer too. It turns out I had liability to consider because I had been relying on aides to do things they aren't supposed to be doing, like dealing with catheters and feeding tubes."

A battle with pneumonia landed Kelly in the hospital earlier in the same year and despite being advised to put Kelly into a nursing home at that time, Brian couldn't do it.

"I just wasn't ready," he said. "In hindsight, I should have done it then. I have always had a hard time telling Kelly 'no' but the time had come."

Brian struggled to talk about the day he took action and moved Kelly to a nursing home in the nearby town of Lowell, Michigan. But battling back emotion, he relayed the day's events of October 7, 2010:

"I had gone to work and returned at around 10 a.m.," he explained. "This was a family decision so Kelly's mom and dad were there. Our nurse's aide left crying because she knew what was happening. Kelly was still in bed and was so excited to see me; then she heard her dad's voice and panicked, thinking that her Grandma Finger had died. She was angry with me as I dressed her and took her to the living room. Then, I just told her I was taking her to a nursing home."

The look of grief on Brian's face told an even deeper story of his personal battle with this decision.

"I thought that her initial diagnosis was going to be the worst time of my life," said Linda. "I was wrong; the worst time was when Brian moved her to the nursing home. I don't blame Brian—he just reached his end."

Kelly described the day as one of the worst of her life and recalls her anger at Brian and the worry over her grandmother:

"I knew my grandmother had not been that well, so I immediately thought something had happened to her," Kelly explained. "Grandma Finger was always so supportive, we had a special relationship and I knew she really loved me."

Brian agreed saying that Grandma Finger was indeed a force of nature.

"Oh, I got the summons," Brian said about going to a family meeting. "When Grandma Finger heard that I had put Kelly in a nursing home, she was angry. She said she had money to pay for a live-in nurse and she'd allow me to live in the basement! So I asked them: what's next? You seem to want to be in charge so are you going to make the next decision? One of you comes to visit on Tuesdays, another of you takes her shopping on Fridays and I appreciate it. But when she needs to be turned over in bed at 3 and 4 and 5 a.m., I'm sure you're all sleeping soundly! None of them stepped up to have Kelly and a nurse move into their homes. After that, they understood, but Grandma Finger didn't and I couldn't help it."

The court of public opinion seems to have passed judgment on Brian, too. Friends and neighbors were shocked by the news and some blamed Brian. Despite his bravado, it's evident that he has heard the comments and felt the pain.

"One friend says that she understands and believes that her own husband would have put her in a nursing home long ago if she were in Kelly's condition. Then another friend squares off and counters that a relationship needs to be stronger, saying that her own husband would never put his beloved in a nursing home." Brian's Irish temper is flaring as he adds, "I'd love to ask her how many times her husband has had to change her tampon... see what she says then."

"Brian is a good guy, he just got worn out," Ron said. "He truthfully felt that he had no choice. We had mixed emotions and felt horrible about this—even suggested getting more help at the house, but we learned that even when extra help was there, Kelly still wanted to rely only on Brian and that just got to be too much. It's sad...if not for the disease, I'm sure they'd be happy and together."

"When I heard the news, I called Brian directly," said Kelly's long-time friend, Traci. "I've known Kelly for over 30 years and Brian for at least 15; I wanted to hear his side of things. When I saw him, I was taken aback by the dark circles below his eyes and how fast he had turned gray. He simply told me that he needed to think of his daughter, that he needed to be around to take care of Rylee."

"Caregiving is a role assumed gradually," said Cindy Streekstra, co-founder of The Caregiver Cottage in Grand Rapids. She and business partner, Carol McGowan are geriatric nurses who specialize in the unique needs of caregivers in their community and have developed cutting-edge services including an adult day program and a telephone support center for caregivers. They also participate in The Caregiver Resource Network of Western Michigan.

"To make time for the tasks that must be handled for the care recipient, the caregiver sacrifices personal time and self care (sleep, grooming, medical/physical needs, diet). The actual emotional relationship between the two people shifts and often suffers," McGowan explained.

"We coach family caregivers to understand that giving care is a job—it needs an actual job description and it's best to separate that job from the relationship," McGowan added. "Also, it's not always *what* you have to do for that person that matters… it's how you *feel* about doing it."

"Each person has his own capacity (emotionally, physically, spiritually) to provide care and tipping points are personal," Streekstra said. "Caregiving can be hazardous to your health and in a way, both the care recipient and the caregiver become victims."

Statistically, that's true. According to the National Family Caregivers Association (NFCA), 40 to 70 percent of family caregivers have clinically significant symptoms of depression while approximately one quarter to one half of them meet the diagnostic criteria for major depression.

The NFCA also states that family caregivers experiencing extreme stress have been shown to age prematurely. This level of stress can take as much as 10 years off a family caregiver's life.

11 Rylee's Turn

"Ever since I was very young, I'd lie down with my mom every night, on her bed," Rylee said. "And if I didn't get to, I'd throw a fit!"

That's a scene that probably sounds hauntingly familiar to many parents leading a very normal life.

"Well, it was always like being a regular family," Rylee recalled. "Mom was home when I'd get off the bus and in the summer, she was always there."

But on the day that Kelly moved to the nursing home, things changed drastically for Rylee.

"I remember getting off the bus and my dad getting home with my grandparents in the car," Rylee said. "Dad and I went into the back yard and he explained that a doctor said Mom would be better off to move out. I asked couldn't Dad do something about it—tell the doctor that Mom is better off here but he said that he couldn't, that this wasn't the first time the doctor had recommended this. It was the first time I ever saw Dad cry. I felt sad, confused and I didn't know what life would be like after that. I went into my room, didn't want to speak to or see anyone, I just hugged my dogs. That night, I couldn't sleep. Usually, Mom was there and I'd sleep with her so I just went to her room and slept in her bed. It was weird—it felt empty."

Although Rylee asked to go see her Mom, Brian explained they needed to wait for a few days—to let Kelly settle in to her new place.

"When we did get to go see Mom, we had to go to that nursing home and it felt just like a hospital," Rylee said. "The smells were bad, the noises were awful and I sure knew I didn't want to bring my friends there—I was embarrassed for her."

Put yourself in Brian's shoes: You've been up since 5:30 a.m., and after getting your family ready for the day, you put in a tough nine hours at work. Then you come home to what you know is going to be a tight schedule—your daughter's band concert is tonight. You walk in to find your father-in-law on the couch, talking with your wife. Your teen-aged daughter and a friend are there too—they need to be at the school early to warm up. Then you notice a puddle under your wife's chair—urine. Your father-in-law says he'll get the girls to the school but that your wife needs some help. Indeed!

So, you physically lift your wife from her wheelchair and carry her into the shower, she needs to be cleaned, her wheel chair needs to be washed and dried, as does the floor. You need to then re-insert her catheter, dress her, comb her hair, clip her finger and toe nails and be at the school within 90 minutes. You miraculously accomplish all of that (having no time to eat any dinner yourself) but instead of a "thank you" you get a sarcastic barb "this is the most attention I've gotten in six months".

How would you feel?

12 A Living Nightmare

The rancid smell of bodily fluids and human waste are overpowering when you walk into the nursing home to see Kelly. It just never smells clean and wafting over it all are the cafeteria smells—truly nauseating. I often sit in my car and gather my courage before trekking into that place to see my friend. I often leave crying for her—at least I can get up and walk out, she is stuck there, stricken by grief.

"Guys just think everything should be easy," Kelly said in anger. "So he thinks… I'll just put her in a nursing home because that'll make things easier for me. I'll come and visit. Well, he didn't talk to me about it beforehand. He still doesn't really know how this impacted me and he won't say much to me about it. But I'm afraid to press it too far…I'm scared he will stop coming to see me, that he'll stop bringing Rylee."

While embarking on a life together, Kelly and Brian talked and planned things together. From the decision to move back to Michigan, to starting a family, building a special house to accommodate her needs, establishing a Special Needs Trust, transferring Power of Attorney and getting a Medicaid Waiver for in-home nursing assistance, they made decisions together. In fact, at least one of these steps landed them, as a couple, in the local daily newspaper, *The Grand Rapids Press*. Their decision making and forethought was lauded in an article on preparedness. Given this pattern, it's no wonder that Kelly was literally shocked by the course of events that left her a virtual prisoner, depending on strangers for even the tiniest of things.

"Looking back I can see I was a pain and pretty demanding," Kelly cried softly. "Now that I'm here and can see how other people are always asking for help, I understand that it's annoying. Just the act of putting chap stick on me is a burden to someone. I had much better care at home. I had an aide - she came to the house 24 hours a week and did things like get me up and dressed in the morning, we got groceries and did laundry. I thought I was contributing at home."

The care provided by one aide to one patient has to be better than the care delivered in a facility where there is sometimes just one nurse to 60 patients and two aides to 30 patients... especially when you consider that Kelly can no longer move any extremities or digits, can't lift her head or even raise her voice.

"I was used to instant gratification at home," Kelly admitted. "I've had to learn to be more patient and to tolerate a lot of discomfort here. Last night I waited for two hours in bed with my call light on before anyone could come to help me. There was just one aide on duty."

Occasionally, friends will drive Kelly back to her house in Belmont, but Kelly says it's painful to go to the home she once loved and to see the dog she misses terribly.

"I was outside the house this week, just looking at it from the driveway and it struck me that Brian can do this without me," Kelly said. "Parenting used to be a big part of my life, now Brian's doing all of that and I am just trying to figure out my new role with Rylee. Brian had claimed that things wouldn't change for me and Rylee when he put me in the nursing home, but now I only get to see her twice a week and we are never alone. That hurts."

Nothing stings quite as much as the feeling of betrayal though, and Kelly's anger over the way Brian handled this life-changing decision is palpable.

"He had a lot of time to consider this while I was just kind of thrown into it. I would have been better off to know how he was feeling and what he was thinking," Kelly said. "In one morning, my life turned upside down. Brian told me he was taking me to a nursing home, he packed my clothes, took me to a doctor who made three random statements, changed the subject and then wanted me to repeat the three random statements. I couldn't do it so he declared me incompetent. That wasn't fair—I was distraught over being taken to a nursing home. Who the hell could pass an acuity test under those circumstances?"

Brian also defended his decision by telling Kelly he was afraid she might harm herself and that his fear was based some of her own comments.

"I know I had made some off-handed comment about taking my chair down some stairs a while ago. It was said in a moment of frustration," Kelly explained. "I never would have done that."

"There were moments when Kelly didn't show the best judgment," Brian said. "Like the day she decided to take the dog for a walk and friends called me because they saw her driving her wheelchair down the center of a busy road with the dog on a leash."

There were other reasons that Brian was concerned for Kelly's well-being and overall health.

"She had lost so much weight, I was worried she was starving to death at home," Brian recalled. "When she went into the nursing home she weighed 89 pounds, largely because she was having nausea from her feeding tube nutrition and frequently asked me to turn it off. At the nursing home, they insisted she take it. They worked out a slow-rate continuous flow and I'm glad. She looks so much healthier now and is closer to her normal body weight."

Days go by and Kelly has acclimated, as much as possible, to her new surroundings. She wrestles with her feelings, seeking to understand why this has happened.

"I know Brian has done a lot for me, my mom even said that he kept me out of a nursing home longer than she could have (mom just physically couldn't provide that level of care)," Kelly said. "And, there were probably so many things that I just didn't realize... he brought it up yesterday and reminded me that he had asked for help. We had agreed that my mom would come to stay over each Wednesday night to give him a break but even when Mom was there, I still called out to Brian in the night. I didn't know how desperate he was. Maybe there were other signs but I just didn't catch on."

Kelly also thought there were many steps to take between being at home and being put in a nursing home.

"I thought we could possibly get additional hours for aides to come in on weekends or even have someone live with us," Kelly said and tears fell. "I also thought that he still loved me and would want me around longer but there have been big changes over the last 10 years. He thought this was the best option for me."

Yet another part of the move to a nursing home had to do with mental acuity and a diagnosis that Kelly challenges.

"I know Brian thought I was forgetting things and that I was messed up in the head," Kelly explained. "He had the doctor test me for Vascular Dementia before bringing me here. Since then, I've mentioned that condition to the psychologist that came to see me on Tuesdays (now a professor at Notre Dame) and she reported that she didn't see any type of dementia."

Imagine sleeping deeply one night and you are awakened by an intense itch on your nose. You desperately need to scratch it but find that you can't raise either arm—it's as if you've been strapped down to your bed and are unable to move or turn over—you can't even wiggle. The itch is awful…you try to turn your head far enough on the pillow to rub the itch away but it is just beyond the height of the pillow's edge. You stick out your tongue trying to stretch it to reach your nose but can't. Wrinkling your nose is ineffective—nothing works to alleviate the discomfort. You call out but no one can hear you over the woman next door incessantly clapping her hands and screaming out for someone to please help her. The tears of frustration streaming from your eyes don't help either. Now you're left with an itch and a puddle to lie in.

13 Rebellion, Acceptance, and Forgiveness

On Tuesdays, Kelly usually sees her friend, Kim Healy, for lunch. On one bright November afternoon I accompanied Kim. As we arrive, aides are busily finishing up Kelly's morning beauty routine, but that doesn't stop us from immediately noticing a new addition to Kelly's face—a small diamond stud pierced through the side of her nose!

"Well, I hadn't experienced that yet so I decided to try it," Kelly says with an impish grin. "I called my cousin and told her I needed a ride to an appointment. I gave her directions while she drove, telling her where to turn. We went to a shop on 28th Street called *Pain for Sale*." I laughed my head off, congratulated her on her bold decision and I told her I admired her spunk!

Others chided her for making such a move.

"It's like I have two teenagers on my hands," Brian said, shaking his head at what he sees as defiance and rebellion.

"Oh, I remember when Kelly got that thing in her nose," Ron said and chuckled. "She kept turning her head this way and that, hoping I'd notice and say something. I saw it alright but I absolutely wouldn't comment on it—it drove her crazy!"

Now and then, Kelly gets an itchy nose and wiggling it helps but sometimes she has to ask for assistance. I have helped her by wiping her nose with a tissue and once I spun the nose ring by accident so the bent post was showing out of the end of her nose.

"Oh, just stick it back in will you?" Kelly said, matter-of-factly and we both chuckled. This is an unconventional relationship with some favors other friends would never ask or need but this is Kelly's normal and I've come to realize that it's just no big deal. She's my friend and she simply has some unique obstacles; she is also very special.

Kelly's roommate is present today, the first time I've seen her in my many visits. She normally is in another wing of the nursing home—being distracted from her battle with dementia. Today, though, it is clear that this poor woman is near death and I am ready to weep for her. Suddenly though, I am taken aback by the mannerisms of the visitor sitting by the woman's bed. This visitor is talking loudly into a cell phone and said, "No, we're here again today, I just don't know what she's holding on for…"

Kelly and I share a frown at the apparent lack of concern for the dying woman's feelings, seeming to share a faith that even near death, or particularly then, we can hear our loved ones. I look to Kelly and feel such sadness for her, because she has had to bear witness to this whole scenario. Then Kelly impresses me yet again, with her spirit of generosity and concern for others.

As we leave the room, she stops to ask me to please open the separation curtain between the two beds so the sunshine will reach the dying woman on the opposite side of the room. Awestruck by Kelly's thoughtfulness, I push the curtain back and for a brief moment, I swear I can see a smile on the woman's face. She died later that evening.

The next week, Kelly gets another roommate but that person is so loud that Kelly can't get any rest. So, there is yet another move. When I visit her in her new room, she is solo for the time being.

"This won't last, there will be someone in here soon I'm sure" Kelly said.

And she is right. Just after the week of the Michigan vs. Michigan State football game, in the fall of 2011, Kelly got a new roommate. But she took it all in stride (or roll) and in fact her mood was bright as she talked about the big game. With a victory for MSU, Kelly won a bet with a therapist who is also a University of Michigan Wolverine fan.

"I went down to the therapy room and my mom helped me to decorate his desk in MSU stuff," Kelly chortled. "I had stickers, crepe paper, curling ribbon and we buried his space in green and white. When he came to work yesterday, he immediately knew who was responsible but what can he do? Later this week he has to wear a green MSU shirt because he lost the bet."

If Kelly could, she would clap with glee. It seems only fair after all—she lost the same bet during basketball season and had to sport the U of M maize and blue!

14 Losing Grandma Finger

Kelly's Grandma Finger died a few short weeks later and feelings of desolation resurged.

"It was devastating…she and I had such a special relationship," Kelly said. "She loved me absolutely and unconditionally; she always made me feel that I was special. I couldn't believe that things could get any worse, but they did."

"Kelly was the first grandchild for my parents and I think she sort of took after my mom (Grandma Finger)," Ron said. "My mom was very independent, always working and doing, she always thought of other people and I think Kelly admired that."

Six months after the death, Kelly received some inheritance. She and Brian had a discussion about it and Kelly told him he should pay off their Belmont home mortgage so that he and Rylee would have that security. And she told him he could use some of it as a down payment on a jeep he'd been wanting.

"Brian came to see me later—he was very quiet. I knew what he was thinking but I didn't *want to know*. I asked him anyway—did he want a divorce," Kelly cried softly. "I told Brian, quite a while ago, that I never wanted to hold him or Rylee back, but when I said that, I didn't mean he should put me in a nursing home and divorce me! Now he wants to start over; he told me that he is only 39 after all!"

"In the year that Kelly had been in the nursing home, we talked repeatedly about the status of our relationship," Brian said. "I know that it's easy to lash out at those closest to you when you are frustrated or in pain but a lot of the time, Kelly could be so mean and I often felt that she despised me. I'm not sure anyone would want to stay married under those circumstances."

"A lot of people suggested I stay married to Kelly and just find a girlfriend," Brian explained. "That wouldn't have been fair to Kelly, any girl I would date, Rylee or myself. I was simply at a point where, as hard as it is to say, I needed to make a clean break and move on."

Brian did stick with the marriage and a worsening situation for over 10 years—that's longer than the average American marriage survives (according to the U.S. Census Bureau). Given that, he is an exception to the statistical trend reported by studies showing that men may just not be destined to be caregivers.

"I know of at least three other women with MS that are in nursing homes," Kelly said. "I also know three men with MS and they are living at home, being cared for by their wives."

According to a November 2009 article in *The New York Times* by Tara Parker-Pope, divorce rates are higher when the wife gets sick.

The article was based on a study conducted by Dr. Marc Chamberlain, a Seattle oncologist, and other colleagues after noticing an alarming pattern—male patients were typically receiving much-needed support from their wives. But a number of female patients were ending up separated or divorced.

The study was based on data gathered on 515 patients who received diagnoses of brain tumors or Multiple Sclerosis from 2001 through 2006. And the results were shocking.

Women in the study were seven times as likely to become separated or divorced as men with similar health problems according to the report published in the *Cancer Journal*.

Overall, about 12 percent of the patients in the study ended up separated or divorced, a rate that was similar to that found in the general American population during that time period (lifetime divorce rates in the United States are higher.) But the pattern changed when the researchers looked at the patient-divorce breakdown by gender. When the man became ill, only three percent experienced the end of a marriage. But among women, about 21 percent ended up separated or divorced.

"All these patients were couples when we met them, but we don't know about pre-diagnosis marital conflicts that had been festering," Dr. Chamberlain said. "The striking part is with life-threatening illness, how often women are abandoned compared to men. That does not speak very well of my gender."

Dr. Chamberlain speculated that differences in male and female roles in the family could explain the trend. "There clearly is an emotional attachment women have to spouse, family and home that in times of stress causes women to hunker down and deal with it, while men may want to flee," he said.

For Kelly, dealing with a divorce is yet another devastating blow and having to tell Rylee was painful.

"I didn't cry," Rylee said. "Most kids hearing about a divorce are upset about the family splitting up and having to live between two houses but my mom was already out of the house. It wasn't really going to change things for me, but I did feel bad for them and I saw how hard it was for my mom."

Given what Kelly has endured over the course of 18 months, it's not surprising that physically, she is losing yet even more ground.

"The stress of all of this emotional upheaval is taking a toll on me," Kelly explained. "And my outlook on the future is different now than when I was at home. I'm exposed to a lot more people here and I worry about getting a cold or pneumonia, which could bring death. I also really worry about talking. If I lose my ability to talk, yet still have all of my thoughts, it would be so horrible."

In a poignant moment of reflection, Kelly wonders if she should have married Brian.

"It's not a question of marrying wrong," Kelly elaborated. "It's a question of whether to have married at all... putting someone in that position...is love enough? After some counseling, I've come to realize that he was a good husband and he took care of me for a long time."

Now the two are trying to settle the divorce and Kelly struggles to keep everything civil. Initially, Brian suggested they share a lawyer to keep costs low but Kelly opted to get her own, deciding it was time to take control over her own destiny. Her first step was to re-assign her Power of Attorney to someone other than Brian. Then she took a hard look at her finances.

"Brian was mad about the amount I wanted in the settlement but I needed to be sure that I look out for my own future and can afford to live. He said that my health isn't good and when I die, the State of Michigan will get the money," Kelly said as she explained how her Special Needs Trust account is structured. "He also feels that he is entitled to more because he took care of me all those years. But looking back on that, it was my SSI benefits that were paying for the house so I can't totally agree with him. And it angers me when people look at me, see I have MS, and act as if I am already dead!"

Kelly does take the latest treatments for MS, saying that it's more about preserving what she's got, so she doesn't lose more function.

"Physically I'm doing OK; my voice has declined a bit but otherwise, my doctors say I'm fine," she said.

15 The Silver Lining in a Very Dark Year

Kelly knew she wanted to find an alternative to the nursing home. It turns out there was a brand new facility, an assisted-living retirement community, just down the road. Each resident moves into a small apartment complete with a separate bedroom, an open floor plan living area that flows into a kitchenette, plus a private, full bath. Each room has a call button to alert nursing staff of any trouble, and there is ample room to accommodate a hospital bed. With caregivers on staff 24/7 and room checks every two hours, this seemed a terrific alternative for Kelly. There is, of course, the issue of cost. The old adage is true...you get what you pay for. The nursing home Kelly was in is a state-regulated facility that accepts Medicaid benefits as its sole payment for services (care rendered). Unfortunately, those funds often leave it understaffed and undesirable.

The new facility, quaintly named Green Acres, will cost additional money—over and above the Medicaid benefit. Kelly remembered working with the Area Agency on Aging once before to get qualified for the MI Choice Medicaid Waiver program which provided her funding for in-home assistance. She called on them for assistance with funding for this new facility and met Amy Cobler, a licensed social worker. Amy turned out to be quite an advocate for Kelly.

MI Choice is a Medicaid-funded program which provides in-home services to older adults and certified disabled individuals who are at risk of nursing facility placement. MI Choice participant facilities partner with a care management team (a licensed social worker and a registered nurse) to develop a care plan centered on an individual's needs.

"MI Choice is now available for assisted living homes - as long as the required qualifications are met," Cobler said. "And it's not just for seniors; it's for adults that are disabled between the ages of 18 and 64 too. It's funded by Medicaid and administered by the Michigan Department of Community Health. Kelly is the perfect candidate for this assistance; and she is so great to work with. I can see that she's not lost anything mentally, she's very sharp. That's the sad thing. She's so young to be so physically limited and yet have normal mental ability—just like you and me. It must be so frustrating for her and I was very pleased to be able to help her."

This was great news for Kelly—coming at a very crucial time!

"The more time I spent over at Green Acres, the less I wanted to be at the nursing home," Kelly said. "I took Rylee over there a few days ago and she sprawled out on the floor— enjoying the nice fresh carpet. That is something I would never allow her to do here—yuk"! Kelly stuck out her tongue for emphasis.

"I had seen Green Acres and in fact, had stopped in to investigate it as an alternative," Brian said. "I inquired about the costs and a Medicaid waiver but at that time, while the facility was just opening, it didn't sound like funding would be available for Kelly—I would have gladly had Kelly be in a nicer place. I'm just very glad it worked out for her."

"At the old place, it always seemed dirty," Rylee said. "Now, at this new place, I feel like I'm at my own house, I throw my stuff down and take off my shoes. And I love having my friends come here too. The people who live here and work here are very nice; it's just a great change."

"A lot of the credit goes to Kelly Ann Marie Johnson at Green Acres," Cobler added. "She really took the initiative to acquire the resources needed for Kelly's care—she dug in and figured it all out. Getting the facility approved to participate in the MI Choice Waiver program takes effort from application to approval—it was really the perfect storm. Kelly reached out at the right time. There was a new facility with vacancy and the right mix of residents—a terrific outcome."

Green Acres is one of 13 assisted living centers owned and operated as part of Retirement Living Management, a family business owned by brothers-in-law Douglas Maas and Paul Wyman. When the new facility opened in Lowell, they already had two residents and had hired a well-qualified manager in Johnson.

While the organizational mission statement focuses on serving seniors, Johnson realized quickly that Kelly needed their services.

"I wanted to be able to help her. I felt for her situation because she is so young and I hated to see her in a nursing home," Johnson said. "I knew also that we could have Rylee come and stay here with Kelly and how critically important that was."

Before taking Kelly on as a resident, the management team had to be assured that staff could fully meet her needs. That included expanding staff, particularly during the midnight shift. It also required substantial new training for the caregivers.

"I had to bring in the right people to educate our staff on everything from feeding tubes to the behavioral issues we might face specifically related to MS," Johnson said. "Kelly's relatively young age was also a concern and the mix of residents had to be considered. The other people here are elderly so we had to ensure that everyone was comfortable with the situation but Kelly fits in extremely well."

Once the decision was made to relocate to Green Acres, Kelly asked for assistance with making lists (she is keenly organized—an expert at utilizing mental notes that is completely amazing). She directs me to a bottom drawer to retrieve a notebook—an MSU green one. So, of course, we discuss the recent football game where a last second play won the day for the Spartans over the Wisconsin Badgers.

Kelly's smile turns to a grimace and she says "I heard about that play but didn't get to see the game; we don't get ESPN here (nursing home)." She then asks me to start a list of follow up questions for Green Acres starting with cable TV...is it included and will she have ESPN?!!

There she goes again, she's about to "just make it happen."

The rest of her list has to do with completely understanding the Medicaid Waiver and just how the money will break down. In the past, Brian had handled those things so now Kelly is seeking the knowledge. There is a vast difference in Kelly on this date—approximately one year after her arrival at the nursing home.

I see the glint of challenge in her eyes. When I compare this new attitude to the constant sheen of tears and utter despair that were clinging to Kelly over the last year, I can nearly sit back and relax with a smile. The relaxation doesn't last long however...there are more lists to make and she is firing items at me in quick, militant style. She is taking charge of the situation.

There is furniture to buy and she knows what she wants: a dining table and chairs (contemporary in style with a rounded rectangular shape), a sleeper sofa with linens for Rylee to sleep on, a TV stand, a dresser…!

"Moving over here to Green Acres has been really, really good for Kelly—it is so much better than where she was before," commented Ron. "And, she got herself here—she found a way to make it happen."

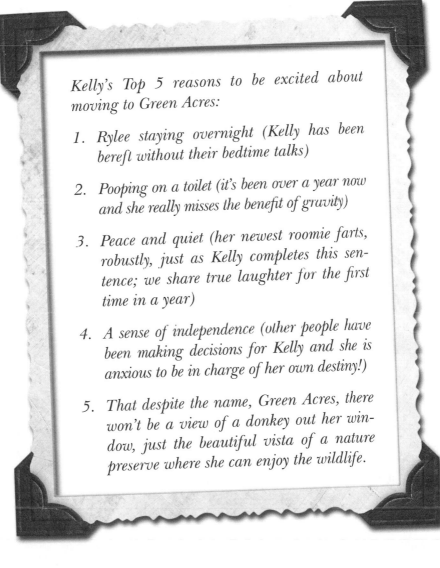

Kelly's Top 5 reasons to be excited about moving to Green Acres:

1. *Rylee staying overnight (Kelly has been bereft without their bedtime talks)*

2. *Pooping on a toilet (it's been over a year now and she really misses the benefit of gravity)*

3. *Peace and quiet (her newest roomie farts, robustly, just as Kelly completes this sentence; we share true laughter for the first time in a year)*

4. *A sense of independence (other people have been making decisions for Kelly and she is anxious to be in charge of her own destiny!)*

5. *That despite the name, Green Acres, there won't be a view of a donkey out her window, just the beautiful vista of a nature preserve where she can enjoy the wildlife.*

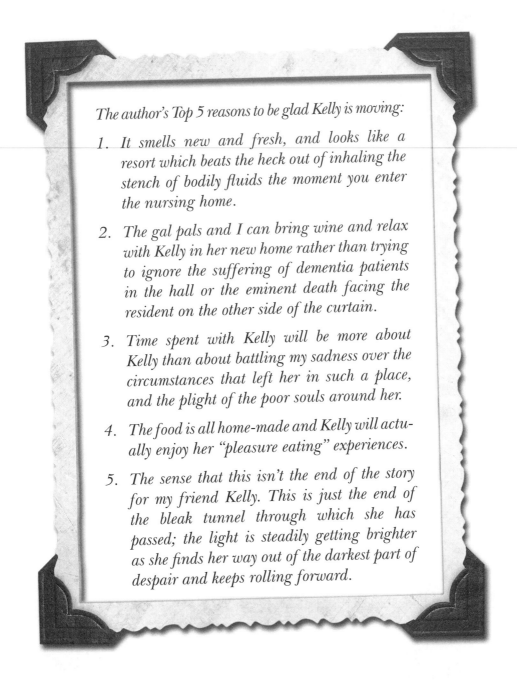

The author's Top 5 reasons to be glad Kelly is moving:

1. *It smells new and fresh, and looks like a resort which beats the heck out of inhaling the stench of bodily fluids the moment you enter the nursing home.*

2. *The gal pals and I can bring wine and relax with Kelly in her new home rather than trying to ignore the suffering of dementia patients in the hall or the eminent death facing the resident on the other side of the curtain.*

3. *Time spent with Kelly will be more about Kelly than about battling my sadness over the circumstances that left her in such a place, and the plight of the poor souls around her.*

4. *The food is all home-made and Kelly will actually enjoy her "pleasure eating" experiences.*

5. *The sense that this isn't the end of the story for my friend Kelly. This is just the end of the bleak tunnel through which she has passed; the light is steadily getting brighter as she finds her way out of the darkest part of despair and keeps rolling forward.*

16 The Big Celebration

Kelly has moved in and we sit comfortably in her stylish new living room. She smiled and recounted her first positive experience at Green Acres.

"I slept like a log—like I haven't in over a year," she said. "It's quiet with no screaming in the night and no miserable alarms going off constantly."

Indeed, the view out her large picture window is of a winter marsh—very serene. Kelly is already planning where to put the bird feeder and has asked me to bring along some power tools next time so we can hang her photo frames and art.

The staff here has made a big difference in Kelly's daily life, too.

"At the nursing home, I'd greet staff with a 'hi and how are you' only to hear that they were counting down the minutes until they could leave work—be done with the job for the day," Kelly said. "Here at Green Acres, it's so much more than that—these people are here because they want to be and the care reflects that attitude."

"The nursing home always seemed dirty, there wasn't enough care and it wasn't the place she belonged," Rylee said. "But here, she's better and it feels like my own house. Plus, I can really talk to my mom now and I can tell her more. At the nursing home, we were never alone and I couldn't say much, but here we can spend time together alone and I can really talk."

I showed Kelly the fun party invitations I picked up at a store recently—thinking that she might want to throw a party for all of her girlfriends. She lights up with excitement at the prospect and we begin the invitation list.

As we set the date, I learn that it will fall on the facility's grand holiday party—complete with a catered dinner and music! The staff assures us that all are welcome, so we keep the date and begin looking forward to seeing about ten of Kelly's closest friends, the Belmont Moms. This is a group of women who formed a friendship after meeting at the local elementary school. Many of them have been asking about Kelly—especially as news spread about the impending divorce and her responding action of moving into a nicer place.

The day of the party, I picked Kelly up early so she could get glammed-up at a salon. Our mutual friend, and very talented beauty professional, Jinnifer Stephan, has offered to do Kelly's make-up and hair for the big event. She looked stunning! Another friend, and professional photographer, Becca Usher lends us her skill to capture each moment of this great celebration.

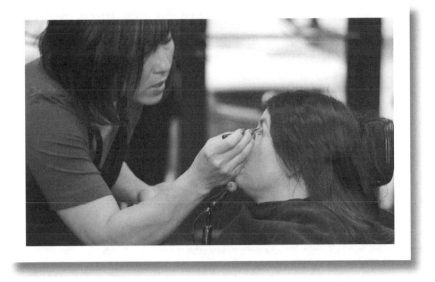

We headed back to party central and Kelly requested some last minute adjustments—clear some clutter and put out the snacks. Guests started arriving and Kelly beamed with pride over her new place—rightly so! It is beautifully decorated and truly reflects her impeccable taste and style. This is not overlooked by good friends and Kelly feels greatly validated, very happy.

Later that evening, I asked her about the importance of girl friends.

"We need the women in our lives," she smiled. "I wish I had more. The best compliment you can give is to tell a girlfriend—I love you like a sister".

Well, her apartment was full of sisterhood tonight!

17 What's in a Purse?

There are people in everyone's life that leave an indelible mark—the type of person that just by living their own life, inspire us to want to emulate them. Kelly has had many loving influencers in her life but one in particular was her Grandma Finger. We were talking about her one afternoon with Kelly's step-sister, Amy Dykstra.

"Grandma Finger was always so thoughtful," Amy said. "She had long relationships, for example, when she and Grandpa would travel, they'd befriend a taxi driver and then continue to keep in touch with him and his whole family, for life."

Kelly has specific memories about the type of person her grandma was too.

"She was always busy, very active and prompt. She didn't forget things like birthdays or what things people liked. She was well-known for her chicken soup - when someone was ill, she'd make up a batch and personally deliver it. Extending a personal touch was very important to Grandma and I'd like to think I'm like her in that way."

Kelly described her grandma's sense of humor as being dry and slightly sarcastic—funny thing, that's exactly how

Kelly described her own sense of humor during an interview over 12 months ago!

Both Amy and Kelly agreed that carrying a big purse was just an extension of Grandma's personality—she wanted to have whatever you might need, at any given time.

What you'd find in Grandma's purse:
- Small sewing kit
- Plastic toothpick
- Lots of pictures
- Eyeglass screwdriver (and extra screws) plus a cleaning cloth
- Kleenex
- Lipstick
- Powder (never lotion or hand sanitizer)
- Chapstick
- Tape measure
- Wallet (always had large bills tucked away in secret places, just in case)
- Small notebook & pen wrapped in a rubber band to keep it closed—it was full of birthdates and special reminders

"Whatever you needed or wanted, she'd give it to you-out of her purse," Kelly joked. "And, if she didn't have what you needed right then, she'd jot it down in her little book and you'd get it later. I learned a lot from my grandma and I've tried to live a little bit like that. It's important for me to pass along these life lessons to Rylee too."

18 Kelly's Epilogue for Rylee

1. Don't judge people by your standards.

2. *Really listen* to people and make mental notes of their likes & dislikes because it makes people feel special.

3. I hope you find happiness by making other people happy.

4. Bad things happen to good people—you don't always get what you deserve. When you don't get what you want, make the best of what you have. Find a way to be happy with it. Happiness is something you make, not something you're given.

5. Don't mix black and navy blue, white and cream or wear dark-colored socks with light shoes. It makes you look gauche.

6. Don't be afraid to admit when you're wrong and apologize when necessary. Be big enough to accept an apology from others too but learn to recognize sincerity—you have to be ready to cut some people loose when they just don't want to stop hurting you. Follow your gut and don't get walked on, you'll know when to end it.

7. Remember that communication is the key to a good relationship. If your significant other gets quiet, don't assume nothing is wrong...ask questions, uncover true feelings.

8. Lastly, I want to tell you something that cousin Jeannie told me at Grandma Finger's memorial. It would be great if you could live by this but it will be hard: Don't cry because it's over...smile because it happened. I'm so thankful for the experiences I've had—graduating high school and college, having a career, a marriage and a child, even navigating a divorce (although I could've done without it). I know some people don't get a chance to do or have all of that. I'm truly grateful and I have Brian to thank for a lot of it.

Kelly has described Rylee as a free-willed person who doesn't always take her advice. Perhaps this list can serve as a compass.

"I really hope Rylee goes on to college but I am not going to push her," Kelly said. "I want her to be a free spirit... with morals."

The Most Amazing Mom

My mom is as creative as an artist,
Making a new master piece.
She's as bright as the sun shining on a
sunny day.
Just like an eight ball, giving me all the
right answers.
My mom is like a warrior,
Fighting through the toughest battles!
Having her in my life
Is like having air to breathe.
She's as special as a person's life to me.
She's like a beautiful flower;
Her cheeks pink like a rose, every hour.
She is like the shining golden sun.
She is really number one!!
Love,
Rylee
2012

19 Those We Can't Live Without

To Kelly, this saying is literal. She knows it and appreciates the key people around her that have loved and supported her her entire life.

A Mother's devotion is often taken for granted or overlooked, but not in Kelly's case. She recognizes that it hasn't been easy for her mom, Linda. Right after Kelly was born, she survived a broken marriage, had to move back in with her father in Belding and find various jobs so her schedule was flexible enough to be a single mom.

She eventually moved herself and Kelly out into an apartment so they could be independent but that was no easier. She then faced the MS diagnosis and treatments while navigating the often difficult mother-daughter angst that comes with the teenage years. Daily life was a virtual roller coaster of emotion… feeling such pride when Kelly was voted homecoming queen and then graduated high school; followed by fear as she ventured out to college with obstacles that others just don't face. Holding Kelly's hand as she lost her hair and bravely endured grueling medical treatments; then celebrating graduation at MSU, followed again by anxiety as Kelly moved to Atlanta for an internship where she was alone for the first time.

Linda felt happiness on Kelly's wedding day, tempered with an underlying concern for the groom; she was excited to jet off to Guatemala to adopt a beautiful granddaughter and happy making the necessary effort to help raise her, often travelling great distances each week to provide care.

This may not be the life Linda dreamed of for her daughter or herself, but she didn't run from it either. She has been unfailing in her support of Kelly.

Grandma Ruth, her mother's mother, has been a force to be reckoned with in Kelly's life as well. Often pragmatic and practical, Grandma Ruth tried to represent reality for Kelly—to caution her about the future when Kelly herself admits that she wasn't looking far down the road. She knew her time would be limited—more than most—and raced to live as fully as possible, hearing Grandma Ruth's advice in her ear all the way. Grandma Ruth was also very generous, renovating a home for Brian and Kelly to live in upon return from Chicago when they were newly married. Then, giving them money for that house when they decided to move to Belmont—helping them to construct a new home that would serve Kelly's special needs as the MS was advancing.

Kelly's Dad has been a constant presence and source of joy in her life too, as has his wife of 27 years, Judi, and her two kids, Matt and Amy. Even now, as adults, Kelly's step brother and sister remain close and involved in Kelly's life.

"Kelly has a unique spirit—she is truly one of a kind," Ron said. "Despite all that she has endured, she has never given up and she doesn't complain—even though she could. Her attitude is so positive...she has made a lifestyle out of making the best of any situation."

"I owe Judi a lot too," Kelly explained. "She exposed me to a lot of new places and things and influenced my ideas about quality—don't settle, keep looking... she introduced me to my favorite store, T.J. Maxx, and we always loved going to the Wealthy Street Farmers Market. I got a neat sun-shaped mosaic wall piece there and have always enjoyed telling friends where I found it—I feel so hip! Judi is definitely always on-trend. But more than that, I learned optimism from her. She always looks for the good in a situation and focuses on moving forward."

20   Live and Learn

While she is feeling more secure and comfortable in her new place, Kelly still has a lot of heartache and is trying to recover from the painful divorce process. Typical Kelly, she is using humor as her chief coping tool.

"Hellooooo," she calls out as I walk into her apartment. "Do I look different?" she asks…I seem perplexed so she fills me in: "I'm single."

This is her way of telling me the divorce is final and she is feeling introspective.

"It's better if you can learn from everything you go through," Kelly said. "And hopefully I've learned not to trust too much, because you just never know. I depended on Brian too much but didn't realize it. Looking back, I know I lost sight of myself. Now that I've taken my life back, I feel pride and I think others respect it too. My big accomplishment was getting out of the nursing home and moving to my new apartment. Truthfully, I was embarrassed to be over there (nursing home) but not here," she smiled brightly. "I feel good about the direction I'm headed."

In her immediate future, Kelly knows she'll be the focus of some extra attention—as this book is released and promoted. It's a strange feeling.

"I tend to be a private person so it's weird, knowing that people will read all this stuff about me," Kelly said. "It's worth it though, if it helps someone... but it's unbelievable to me, that the things I did could actually help someone else—it wasn't calculated, it's just how I lived."

Helping others is on the top of the agenda (both Kelly's and mine) as we make plans to go to press with this story. We definitely want to use a percentage of net book sales to make a difference.

"Green Acres is terrific and I know how lucky I am to live here—to have received the sort of funding that I qualified for," Kelly said. "But I really wish there was an assisted living center for younger people. There just isn't anything like that around here, so maybe we could raise money to develop something like that?"

Interestingly, Kelly's idea is in sync with a current trend.

According to the U.S. Centers for Medicare and Medicaid Services, over the last ten years, adults ages 31 to 64 have been the fastest growing population in nursing homes. Kelly is part of that trend.

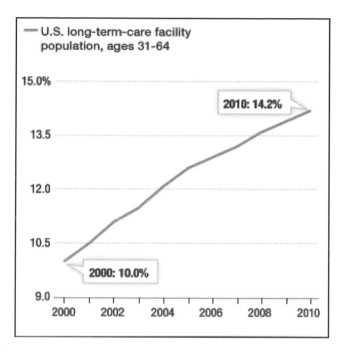

Source: U.S. Centers for Medicare and Medicaid services
Credit: Robert Benincasa and Stephanie d'Otreppe / NPR

There indeed seems to be a need for alternatives; our work isn't done! I smile at her moxie, I always will when I think back on our time together, writing this story—The Kelly Finger-McNeela story.